BUSTER'S LOST MOSHLINGS:

A Search-and-Find Book

Last night, as I was snoozing after a long day's Moshling hunting, something terrible happened. Dr. Strangeglove broke into my secret ranch and he's let all my Moshlings escape! Can you help me round up the crazy critters?

Ooh La Lane

Here I am outside the Googenheim on Ooh La Lane, but there's no time to check out the art or pop into Gabby's for a cuppa today. I gotta find my little friends!

Can you find . . . ?

- Hansel
- Grigi
- Scamp
- Lady Meowford
- Squidge

Main Street

This ain't no time for a picnic, we got Moshlings to catch. With that seed cart here, those itty bitty beasties can't be too far away!

Can you see . . . ?

Jeepers

Peppy

Fumble

Dipsy

Snookums

Down at the Port

Gee wiz, that's quite a hike from Main Street to the Port, but I'm determined to find those pesky Moshlings. Maybe Lefty can keep a look-out for me from the crow's nest . . .

Can you spy . . . ?

- ShiShi
- Prof Purplex
- Cali
- I.G.G.Y
- Doris

Going Underground

Searching the sewers ain't my kind of fun, but tracking Moshlings is, so here I am. Don't get me wrong, I ain't afraid of getting mucky, but it sure does stink down here!

Can you see . . . ?

Cutie Pie

Angel

Fifi

Purdy

Ecto

The Underground Disco

There sure was a big queue, luckily I had my Moshi Passport on me to get in! Moshlings do love to boogie, so I bet they're jigging around in here somewhere . . .

Can you spot . . . ?

Roxy

Sooki-Yaki

Rocky

Humphrey

Tiki

Simon Growl's Mansion

Barbecued bubblefish, have I got my work cut out for me or what? Simon Growl's humongous house has loads of places for those teeny weeny tykes to hide out!

Can you find . . . ?

Stanley

Honey

Shelby

Gurgle

GROWL MANSION
Wipe your feet

Puzzle Palace

Just takin' a quick break to give these guys some maze-solving tips. We're gonna need them to search this puzzling palace!

Can you find . . . ?

Burnie

DJ Quack

Lady GooGoo

Flumpy

Pooky

At the Beach

Oh, I do like to be beside the seaside,
oh I do like to be beside the sea . . .
Buckets and spades, where can those
Moshlings have got to?

Can you dig up . . . ?

Cleo

Chop Chop

Kissy

Gingersnap

ICE-SCREAM

GG1

Roary Scrawl's House

Roary's always got his eyes at hand for a top ooze story, maybe he can lend me a couple to seek out those cheeky little chums of mine . . .

Can you find . . . ?

Coolio

Priscilla

White Fang

Liberty

Moshi Fun Park

So many distractions at the Moshi Fun Park, but I have to round up the rest of my critter collection. Maybe I'll just have a quick spin on the Octo-Whirl and see what I can spy from up there . . .

Can you see . . . ?

General Fuzuki

Blurp

Blingo

Mini Ben

Buster's Ranch

Home sweet home! I hope my last few Moshlings have got away from that creepy Dr. Strangeglove and made it back safely . . .

Can you spot . . . ?

Oddie

Mr Snoodle

McNulty

Waldo

Big Bad Bill

Search and Find!

Just in case you need a little reminder, here are all my missing Moshlings to look out for on each spread:

Jeepers | ShiShi | Humphrey | Burnie

Peppy | Prof. Purplex | Tiki | DJ Quack

Fumble | Cali | Stanley | Blurp

Dipsy | Iggy | Honey | Flumpy

Snookums | Doris | Gurgle | Pooky

Sooki-Yaki | Chop Chop | Shelby | General Fuzuki

Rocky | Cleo | Liberty | Mini Ben

Hansel | Cutie Pie | Oddie | Coolio

Grigi | Angel | Mr Snoodle | Priscilla

Scamp | Fifi | McNulty | White Fang

Lady Meowford | Purdy | Waldo | Gingersnap

Squidge | Ecto | Big Bad Bill | Kissy

Blingo | Lady Goo Goo | Roxy | ?

Hmm, there's gotta be another secret Moshling out there to complete the set. I sure hope I find it soon...

I always take my camera Moshling hunting with me, you never know what you might spot! See if you can work out where I took these sneaky snapshots!

Did you notice the latest addition to my secret Moshling set, Blingo? You can add him to your collection too, with this unique code! Use a mirror to reveal the code, then enter it on the sign-in page of **moshimonsters.com**. But beware, **every code is different** - don't share the secret with your friends, as **it will only work once!**

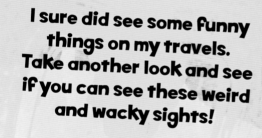

I sure did see some funny things on my travels. Take another look and see if you can see these weird and wacky sights!

1. DJ Quack in a gas mask
2. A mushroom on a firework
3. Raarghly with a present
4. Waldo wearing ear plugs
5. A rug with eyes
6. Dipsy waterskiing
7. Katsuma Krunch cereal
8. Hansel playing a banjo
9. General Fuzuki riding a cow
10. Roary with some roses
11. Squidge with a gold hoop earring
12. A red snoring hickopotamus
13. Jeepers building a sandcastle
14. Tamara Tesla electrocuting Gurgle
15. 37 Rox in the Puzzle Palace
16. 54 Flutterbys on Main Street
17. Chop Chop wearing a blue bandana
18. 58 mushrooms outside the Disco
19. Myrtle with a treasure chest
20. Burnie setting fire to Stashley Snoozer's hat
21. 20 ice creams at the beach
22. Beau Squiddley catching an Oddie

ALSO
AVAILABLE: